Mother of a Mystic

The Life of Anna Columbia Heath Holmes

ADDITIONAL BOOKS BY

MARILYN LEO

In His Company: Ernest Holmes Remembered

EDITOR, *Love and Law*

Chronicles of Religious Sciences, Volumes I and II

CONTRIBUTOR, *Conversations with Ernest*

CONTRIBUTOR TO MAGAZINES, INCLUDING *Science of Mind,
Creative Thought,
International New Thought Alliance*

Mother of a Mystic

The Life of Anna Columbia Heath Holmes

BY MARILYN LEO

FOREWORD BY
JESSE JENNINGS, D.D.

Park Point Press | 573 Park Point Drive | Golden CO 80401-7042

Park Point Press
573 Park Point Drive
Golden, CO 80401-7402
720-496-1370
www.csl.org/en/publications/books
www.scienceofmind.com/publish-your-book

Published December, 2020

Editor: Julie Mierau, JM Wordsmith
Design/Layout: Maria Robinson, Designs On You, LLC

ISBN ebook: 978-0-917849-90-9
ISBN paperback: 978-0-917849-89-3

Dedication

TO OUR MOTHER, whose gentle manner covered a brilliant mind that she dedicated to the service of her sons and the church, and to her leadership in far-flung charities, for all of which she became known among millions as "Mother Holmes."[1]

— Fenwicke L. Holmes

Foreword

WHAT SWEET SYMMETRY there is in this author select-
ing her subject. Rev. Dr. Marilyn Leo is very much the matriarch
of today's Religious Science, Centers for Spiritual Living students
and communities, as was Mother Holmes over her many years.

Dr. Leo's deep research, carefully and warmly set out, weaves
several tales. We learn of generations of a north woods farming
family, whose attention had to be on sustenance and even sur-
vival, but extended further into shaping their children's destinies
through education and daily spiritual practice. We peek into a
time unimaginable to most of us (nine days to travel across a small
state!), then follow the characters as they enter the modern era
with their common sense and work ethics intact. We discover the
"tough love," practical and philosophical yet seldom sentimental,
that basically forged the mystic Ernest Holmes, whose writings
I treasure and precepts I follow.

Hard work made Ernest what he would become to the world, family bonds sustained him through both towering achievements and bitter disappointments, but there was one particular gift I believe most of all lit his way, and it came from his mother. Alongside father William, Anna Holmes taught the brothers not to fear God but to feel God's love and to go forward with optimism and enthusiasm.

Anna Holmes knew without question that with God all things are possible, even the healing of this world.

Jesse Jennings, D.D.
October 20, 2020

Preface

WRITING THIS STORY has been both an informative and a delightful journey through the life of Anna Columbia Heath Holmes. I was a young girl when I knew her and, of course, I knew her only as "Mother Holmes."

As I read the different accounts of Anna's life and personality, I would chuckle, as everyone's accounts are from their own memories and perceptions of circumstances. People living the same story or incident may have a different view and tale accordingly.

So this process has been interesting, challenging, and fun. I am grateful for the opportunity.

— Marilyn Leo

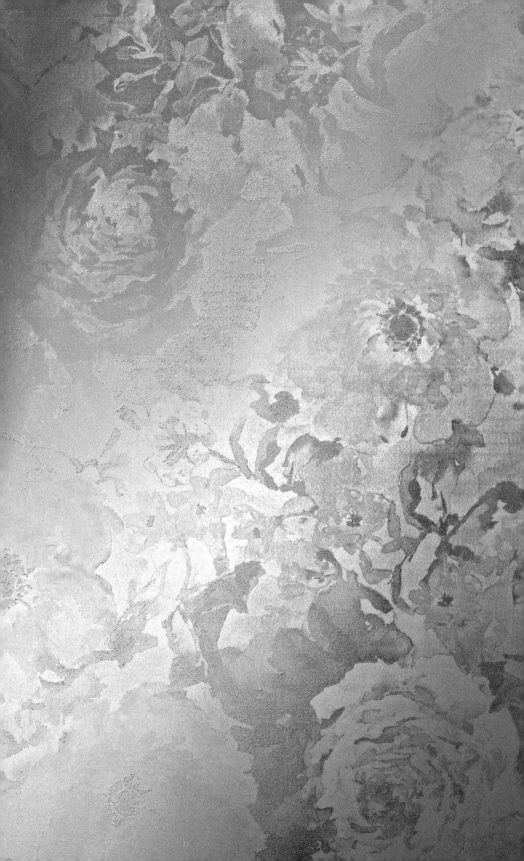

Acknowledgments

I WOULD LIKE TO FIRST THANK James van Cleave, Ph.D., President of the Science of Mind Archives and Library Foundation, for the great interest he had in Anna Columbia Heath Holmes, affectionately known as "Mother Holmes," after reading the article "Zest for Living" by Cheerio Meredith in the *Science of Mind* magazine. Anna was the mother of Ernest S. Holmes, well-known and beloved lecturer and healer in the early 20th century, and also seven more successful sons. Thank you, too, to Rev. Kathy Mastroianni, Executive Director of the Archives, for her assistance in sending me the necessary letters, pictures, and other papers for this book, assisted by Archives volunteer Rev. Dr. Kathleen Lenover. And for the loving encouragement and support of friends, *thank you.*

Marilyn

Remember... the movies of pioneers

coming across the plains and over

the Rocky Mountains? It took strong, determined

people to make that trip. I'm not saying

that Anna Holmes was on one

of those trips in a covered wagon.

No, the petite matriarch of the family waited

several years and traveled across the

continent in more comfortable surroundings, by train.

But wait, we're getting ahead of the story . . .

Table of Contents

PHOTOGRAPHS & ILLUSTRATIONS
pages 2, 11, 12, 13, 14, 20, 22, 28, 35, 37, 43, 48, 49, 50, 53, 54, 56, 58, 59,
61, 63, 64, 69, 97

About This Book

INFORMATION FOR THIS BOOK came from a variety of sources, including: *Ernest Holmes: His Life and Times* by Fenwicke L. Holmes, son of Anna; "Zest for Living" by Cheerio Meredith, *Science of Mind* magazine, August 1947; *Jerome Holmes' Ancestry Journal,* gifted to me from Fenwicke William, the son of Jerome Crane, son of Anna; *That Was Ernest* by Reginald Armor; a taped interview between the author and Reginald Armor in 1975; additional information found in the Science of Mind Archives; and the author's memory.

As noted in the book, there have been questions of some dates and places between Fenwicke Lindsay, son of Anna, and author of *Ernest Holmes: His Life and Times,* and her grandson Fenwicke William, *Jerome Holmes' Ancestry Journal.*

The Life of Anna Columbia Heath Holmes

Chapter One

If, in 1947 or before, you had been invited to a party at the home of Ernest and Hazel Holmes on "The Hill," you would most likely encounter a lovely elderly lady sitting in a grand chair watching and enjoying the fun of the event. She may even be knitting, for she was known to always having knitting needles and yarn in her hands or nearby. This beautiful lady is Mother Holmes, as she was affectionately called, and in that year she would have been nearly ninety-six years of age.

Her Childhood Years

Anna Columbia Heath was born January 1, 1851, in the village of Oxford, Maine. She came from a long line of Scottish and English people; eight families were known to have come to America on the Mayflower. As was common at the time, there is some disagreement as to the year of Anna's birth. Therefore, her age in 1949, the year of her transition, would be ninety-eight, not ninety-nine, as believed for these many years.[2]

Let's begin this story imagining a petite woman in the late 1800s with a slight build but solid muscle, strong enough to handle most any situation that her nine sons and a farm in Maine might present. She did not travel across the plains and Rocky Mountains of America until many years later but had the work ethic and stamina of one who might undertake that journey in a covered wagon.

Anna's grandfather, James Sullivan Heath Sr., built a gristmill in the village of Oxford, Maine, to grind corn and wheat and to serve the community in this capacity. It was a successful and lucrative business. His son, James Heath Jr., at age sixteen was sent off to Bridgeton Academy for a four-year education with the expectation that he would one day run the mill.

When his father passed on, James Jr. inherited one half of

the family's assets and the mill. At about that time he began court-
ing Jennette Ryerson. They were married but not long after the
ceremony, and Anna's birth to the young 17-year-old bride, James
Jr. decided he would rather sail west in search of gold.

Once he boarded the ship, he was not heard from again. His
disappearance remains a mystery. However, it is recorded that he
died on his journey to California on February 16, 1852. Jennette
was left to run the mill and be a mother on her own.

When Anna was six years old she was sent to Lincoln, Maine,
with her father's brother, Uncle Jacob. Her mother, Jennette, was
to remain in Oxford to continue to run the mill. Anna and her
uncle finally arrived after traveling by horse and buggy for nine
days and 365 miles to "The Neighborhood" in Lincoln. Anna's new
home was a big white house on a hill surrounded by maple trees
and fields of grass.

In this home for the next six years Anna would learn the
Scottish way of life and endless activity. From early morning until
bedtime even young Anna had chores such as peeling apples,
sweeping, dusting, helping to prepare meals, washing dishes, and
the many other daily activities for a young girl to perform. In addi-
tion there was always sewing and mending, knitting mittens and
socks. These were the activities of Anna's early days and they
continued in this manner throughout her life. In later years you
most always would see knitting needles and yarn in Anna's hands.

When Anna was eleven her mother sold the mill in Oxford
and moved to Lincoln to be near her daughter. Within two years
Jennette met Winborn Pinkham and married him. They had two
sons, Fred and Henry. Pinkham, Anna's new stepfather, had a

farm near the Heath property, and at age thirteen Anna went to live with her new family and help her mother care for the two boys.

After a couple of years Anna, believing there was to be more to her life and wanting to be educated, enrolled in the local institution of Mattanawcook Academy. She studied for six years and became a schoolteacher. "...[S]he developed the art of speech and diction and the three R's and became the best speller in that part of Maine."[3]

Even though Anna was small in stature, she had a manner about her of confidence and firmness such that no boy in her schools was unruly or bold with her more than once. She could handle any circumstance.

Anna had blue eyes and reddish-blond hair that hung down to the floor. She put her hair into braids and wound them around her head. She had a whimsical smile. Son Fenwicke described his mother this way: "In the history of faiths, Mother's name will someday be written beside those other mothers, Santa Monica and Susannah Wesley. Her faith in the Immediate presence of God, her intellect, her originality, and her administrative capacity were respected and admired among not only the common people of our boyhood but also the learned and prominent, and in social service circles in the last third of the century of her life... ."[4]

Chapter Two

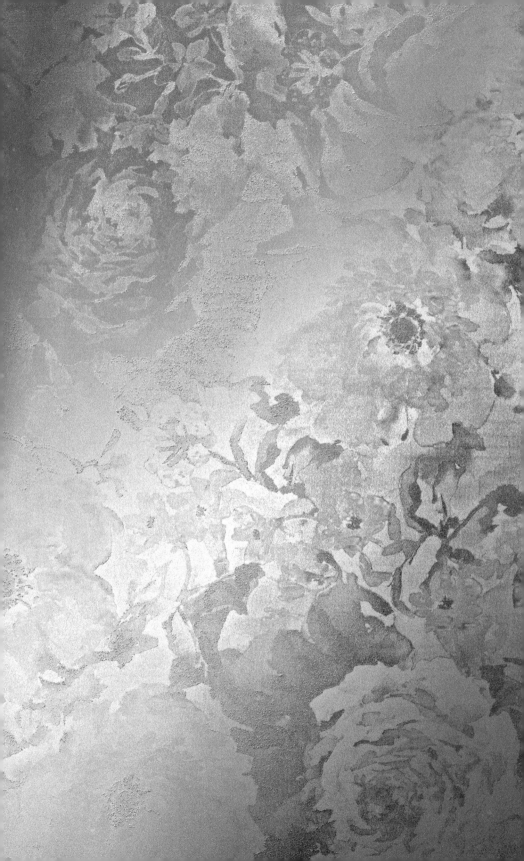

Her Courtship & Marriage

William Nelson Holmes was the seventh of twelve children. He was born April 7, 1846, into the Daniel Holmes family in Petitcodiac, Canada, and his ancestry was traced back to an English aristocrat, Sir William Ketchum.[5] Historians have some disagreement as to William Nelson's birthplace, as the *Holmes' Ancestry Journal* places his birth in the village of Salisbury, New Brunswick. Perhaps the birth records were kept in a different village.

William Nelson "...was rather on the dreamy side of life, full of fun and imagination, but proud of his ability as a wrestler and able to throw any man in the neighborhood in spite of his slight stature."[6]

He was the most scholarly of his siblings, and his family planned for him to have a complete education. Instead, at age fourteen, he ran away and was not in touch with his family for several years. He also changed his name, which later was to become a deterrent to marriage with Anna Columbia Heath.

William at age seventeen worked on the farms near Lincoln, Maine. He saved his money and bought a farm near the Winborn Pinkham farm, where thirteen-year-old Anna came to live with her mother and stepfather.

In time, William and Anna met and began their long conversations, finding they had much in common and lots to talk about in regards to crops and farming in general. They were not always in agreement on farming tactics, making for long and diligent discussions on ways to preserve and use the soil.

William came to adore Anna and wanted to marry her, but before she would say yes, she was determined that William should write to his parents and use his legal name. When he left home, he assumed a different name. William left his farm and Anna, going to live with his sister in a Dutch community of Pennsylvania, where he learned to speak, read, and write the language. He already had easily mastered French on his own and had some knowledge of Latin and Greek roots.

William finally returned home and wrote a letter to his parents in Petitcodiac to inform them he would soon be bringing his bride home to meet them.

They were married in November 1875. Anna was twenty-five years of age.

The newlyweds went to New Brunswick, Canada, to meet William's family—but Anna was upset that her twenty-eight-year-old husband was called Willie, a nickname for a child. Anna wanted to return home to The Neighborhood and so they did—in time for the birth of their first son. During the next eleven years, eight more boys would follow: Walter, Luther, William, Charles, Harry (died in infancy), Fenwicke, Guy, Jerome, and Ernest Shurtleff, in that order. All were born at home with the assistance of a midwife. Anna was thirty-seven years of age at the time of Ernest's birth.

The young Holmes family lived on the border of the "Habitant Country." The indigenous tribes of Canucks and Penobscot lived nearby. The winters were harsh and the land had to be cleared of rocks before fields could be planted.

William Nelson Holmes and Anna Columbia Heath may have been stern, but they were loving parents. They taught their boys to work hard, as Anna had been taught, and to love God.

Anna Columbia Heath
Holmes and her husband William Nelson Holmes

Pedigree of Anna Columbia Heath

Paternal Grandmother
of Fenwicke William Holmes

GRAND	GREAT (1)	GREAT (2)	GREAT (3)	GREAT (4)	GREAT (5)

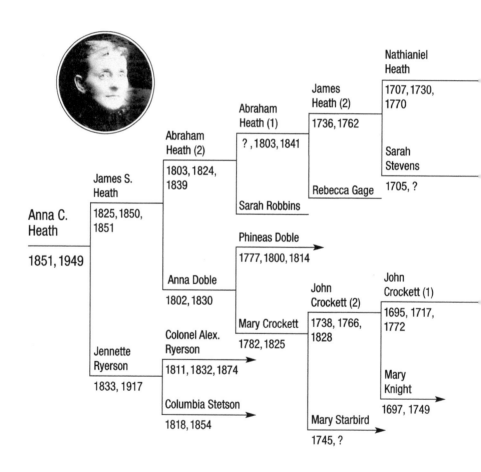

Nathianiel
Heath

1707, 1730,
1770

James
Heath (2)

1736, 1762

Abraham
Heath (1)

?, 1803, 1841

Sarah
Stevens

1705, ?

Rebecca Gage

Abraham
Heath (2)

1803, 1824,
1839

James S.
Heath

1825, 1850,
1851

Sarah Robbins

Anna C.
Heath

1851, 1949

Phineas Doble

1777, 1800, 1814

John
Crockett (1)

1695, 1717,
1772

Anna Doble

1802, 1830

John
Crockett (2)

1738, 1766,
1828

Mary Crockett

1782, 1825

Colonel Alex.
Ryerson

1811, 1832, 1874

Jennette
Ryerson

1833, 1917

Mary
Knight

1697, 1749

Columbia Stetson

1818, 1854

Mary Starbird

1745, ?

GREAT (5)	GREAT (6)	GREAT (7)	GREAT (8)	GREAT (9)	GREAT (10)

Nathianiel Heath

- James Heath 1683, ? , 1758
  - Josiah Heath 1651, 1671
    - Bartholemew Heath 1615,1640,1681
      - Joseph Moyce 1585, 1609
    - Hannah Moyce 1618, 1655
      - Hannah Folcord ? , 1655
  - Mary Davis 1647, >1691
    - Ens John Davis 1623, 1646, 1686
      - James Davis 1583,1618,1678
        - John Tayer bp 1561, 1589,
      - Cicely Tayer bp 1600, 1673
        - Joan Lawrence 1570, ?
- Mary Bradley 1671, 1718
  - Daniel Bradley
  - Mary Williams
    - Jane Peasley 1630, ?
      - Joseph Peasley ? , 1600
        - John Johnson
      - Mary Johnson
        - Mary ?

Sarah Stevens

- Samuel Stevens ? , 1704,
  - John Heath 1643,1666,1706
    - Bartholemew Heath 1615,1640,1681
      - Joseph Moyce 1585, 1609
    - Hannah Moyce 1618, 1655
      - Hannah Folcord ? , 1655
- Rachel Heath 1682, ?
  - Sarah Partridge 1647, 1718
    - Wiliam Partridge
    - Ann ?

John Crockett (1)

- Joshua Crockett 1650, 1719
  - Thomas Crockett (2) 1610, ? , 1677
    - Thomas Crockett (1)
    - Ann ?
  - Anna Lynn 1617, 1713
    - Henry Lynn
    - Sarah Tilley
- Susan Trickey 1661, 1731
  - Thomas Trickey
  - Elizabeth ?

Mary Knight →

Nathan Knight

THE HOLMES COAT OF ARMS HEREBY ILLUSTRATED IS OFFICIALLY DOCUMENTED IN BURKE'S GENERAL ARMORY, THE ORIGINAL DESCRIPTION OF THE ARMS (SHIELD) IS AS FOLLOWS:

"BARRY OF EIGHT OR AND AZ, ON A CANTON GU. THREE GARLANDS PPR."

WHEN TRANSLATED THE BLAZON ALSO DESCRIBES THE ORIGINAL COLORS OF THE HOLMES ARMS AS:

"DIVIDE INTO EIGHT HORIZONTAL BARS, GOLD AND BLUE; ON A RED UPPER CORNER THREE NATURALLY COLORED GARLANDS,"

ABOVE THE SHIELD AND HELMET IS THE CREST WHICH IS DESCRIBED AS: "A GOLD LION'S HEAD PLACED VERTICALLY."

Chapter Three

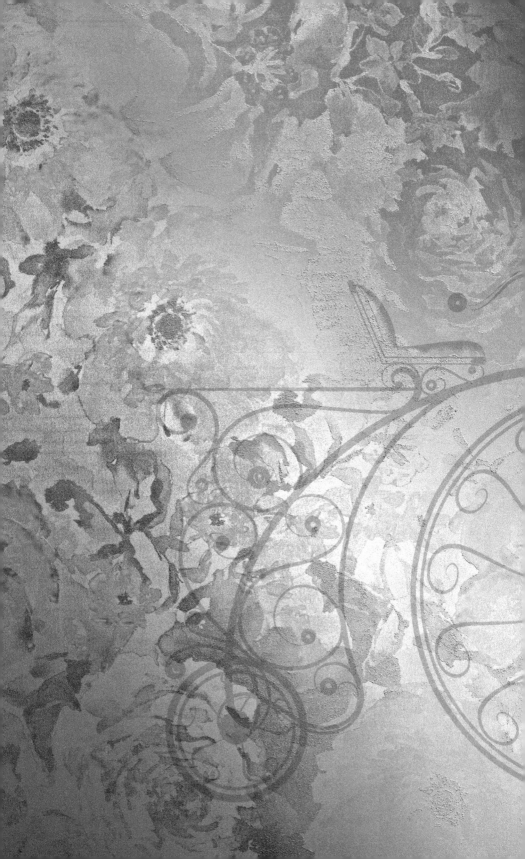

Her Family Life

Rev. Ernest Warburton Shurtleff, 1862-1917, was an itinerant minister who traveled the countryside on his bicycle with the big six-foot wheel. He visited the Holmes family regularly and would spend many hours in conversation and discussion about the Bible with Anna. She held deep respect for him and when it was time for the newest offspring to be named, she decided on Ernest Shurtleff.

Shurtleff was later known for his volumes of poetry and other classics. He became a popular Congregational minister and was probably best known for his writing of the hymn, "Lead On, O King Eternal."

Some six years later, in Bethel, there was another minister, Reverend Farley, who often visited the Holmes family. He realized Anna's great intellect and education and enjoyed their discussions and listening to her point of view. Of course, both Anna and William were diligent in counteracting the religious teachings of dualism, good and evil.

Each day in the Holmes' home, the Bible was read at the kitchen table. William and Anna were both of the thinking that it was best to teach the boys optimism rather than fear when it came to the teachings in the Bible. So hell and damnation and the idea of being worms of dust had no place in their studies.

There were always books in the home and a library where they could borrow other books. Time for reading was always important, including sharing bedtime stories from *Children's Bible Story Book*. She believed these stories had a great influence on the lives of little children and selected particular stories because of their emphasis on faith and omitting fear. She was always trying to protect their young minds from fear.

She remembered that in her childhood there was always more fear than love taught in the church. But there was also great faith. In a young mind, there is usually exaggeration and her opinion was that it was unhealthy to teach fear all the time.

Ernest seemed to be the most spiritually in tune with Anna. Because he was her "baby," along with his extreme curiosity about all of life and nature—and his sensitivity, his mother seemed to recognize a need for him that she could fulfill. They were very close throughout her life.

As the boys grew, they each had chores and all joined in the effort to remove the glacier rocks that popped up in the soil. There was much to be done on the farm near the village of Lincoln and they all pitched in. Even the youngest would help by setting the table for meals.

Seven of the boys took to farming, as did other farm boys living nearby. But Ernest, the youngest, was different and his parents sensed it. He was full of curiosity for life and wanted to know what made everything work. This great inquiring mind began in infancy, and his curiosity for all things remained throughout his life.

Over the years the family moved many times, as William needed to find employment. The whole family would remain together and move wherever they needed to be.

A typical day on the Holmes farm would begin at 3:30 in the morning when William would get up to begin his day. By daybreak Mother, Anna, would be up preparing breakfast for the boys. Her day might include making soap out of animal fat and the lye collected from ashes. She would sit on a three-legged stool at her spinning wheel and spin wool into yarn or weave rag rugs after the boys had torn rags into strips, sewed the ends together, and wound them into a ball. She might feed the chickens and livestock and, of course, care for her boys, making their clothes or mending them, working in the garden for fresh produce, cleaning the house, and preparing meals. And when needed, on the farm you could find her planting seed and helping wherever possible.

There were many more chores that continued into the evening and after everyone else had gone to bed. Anna loved the still of the night and would often sit and contemplate the universe. She was well acquainted with the stars and planets and could name many of them.

Anna had a favorite barrel chair that had been made by cutting away half of the upper part of a barrel and stuffing the

Standing left to right: Luther, Charles, Fenwicke, William and Walter
Seated left to right: Jerome, Mother Holmes, Ernest (about eight years
old), William Sr. (Father), and Guy

lower half with straw covered by a cushion. It was here, sitting by the fire, you would probably find her knitting, darning, or reading. It was here she nursed her babies for their first year of life.

The boys kept busy with school and chores on the farm—and you might think they were perfect angels, never making mischief. You would be wrong. They were normal farm boys, loving to play and looking to find themselves something special to do. But Anna never spanked them for wrongdoing. No, she knew many appropriate stories, usually in verse, that would get the moral lesson across.

Anna loved her sons deeply but she was not sentimental—she never shed tears but permitted a "flitting kiss" from each boy at bedtime. The day Fenwicke broke his arm, Anna tied him to her so that the rough ride in the buggy to the doctor would not be so painful.

Anna loved poetry and often read aloud. Ernest loved to hear the poetry and after hearing a particular poem a few times would soon be able to quote from memory. He would continue to do this throughout his life.

Before Ernest was old enough to attend school he would tag along after his brothers and sit and listen to what they were learning. Even though he never attended The Gould Academy for higher education with his brothers, his love of study and learning stayed with him throughout his life. All of the boys loved to read and they read anything they could get their hands on, including magazines, books on travel, mythology, the old west, hunting, Indian stories, adventures, and others, some as old as fifty years. Anna was known as "the mother of those children who are always toting books."[7]

One time she discovered a couple of the boys reading Peck's *Bad Boy*, a book they had bought and read at night, under the covers. When she found it, Anna took tongs to pick up the book and throw it into the fire. With that, as happens with most children, all the boys chipped in to buy another copy.

Ernest would devour such authors as Lowell, Longfellow, Holmes and such books as *The Iliad, The Odyssey,* and *Last Days of Pompeii*. His photographic memory led him to memorize and recite great poetry, such as *Hiawatha* and Rudyard Kipling's *Mother O'Mine.*

As a minister and lecturer, many years later, every Mother's Day, Ernest would recite from the lectern with great dramatic fervor, with tears for emphasis:

> If I were hanged on the highest hill,
>   Mother o'mine, O mother o'mine,
> I know whose love would be with me still,
>   Mother o'mine, O mother o'mine.
>
> If I were drowned in the deepest sea,
>   Mother o'mine, O mother o'mine!
> I know whose tears would come down to me,
>   Mother o'mine, O mother o'mine!
>
> If I were damned of body and soul,
> I know whose prayers would make me whole,
>   Mother o'mine, Ooooo mother o'mine!

ODE TO ERNEST

I'm damn near dead the old stork said
As he dumped his bundle on the bed.

I've traveled this route till I'm all tired out
Am beginning to wonder what it's all about.

This is my last trip, I hope not my worst,
For in that bundle there ain't weinerwurst.

To make this one, I used up my scraps
He may turn out all right - he will, perhaps.

I couldn't make him tall, so I made him wide,
What talents to give him I couldn't decide.

So I threw in a little of this and a little of that,
I had so much lard, I'm afraid he'll be fat.

I hadn't much hair, but a lot of nose
He'll look kinda funny, I suppose.

I made his head, put on eyes and ears
Than I was really shaken with doubt and with fears.

I had nothing left to put inside
I had to hurry or the child would have died.

So I dumped into the head the junk I had
Some must have been good, but the rest was bad.

There were a few facts, some fancies, a gadget or two
Some few scattered brains, but

Then I got scared and slapped on the lid
And out of the chimney quickly I slid.

Then I let go, and let God do it.
I hope to heavens he won't rue it.

The years have gone by - he hasn't been too bad
He's done all right - with the brains he had.

He didn't grow tall - but he did grow wide
What he was to be, he had to decide.

Whether a merchant, a barber, a plumber, a thief
Whatever it was, he'd have to be chief.

So he studied and conjured - thought and conjoled
He wanted to be a preacher - if the truth must be told.

So he hired him a hall - put on a long gown
And before we could believe it - he was de lux, renown

Time went on for quite a spell
The first thing he did was put out the fire in hell.

Then he created a heaven - right inside each guy
Spent all his time - explaining just why.

Everywhere he went, he cast a spell
And soon everybody agreed there was hell.

Eat, drink and be merry was what he taught
But not too much of either - it was balance he sought.

So now he is an old man - has done the best he could
And acted generally like a good preacher should.

So let's drink to the stork who kept on trying
For he made a darn good finish - that's no lying.

"TO ERNEST ON HIS BIRTHDAY: 'SILVER AND GOLD HAVE I NONE.
SUCH AS I HAVE I GIVE UNTO YOU.' READ ALONE."
This was attached to a typed poem presumably written by Anna Holmes,
date unknown.

As his recitation continued, you could see tears running down his cheeks and with great dramatic gestures and pointing to the sky he would come to the end, and just at the right moment, pull a large white handkerchief from his pocket and quietly say, "Isn't it terrible to see a fat man cry?" This immediately changed the atmosphere to joy, and the audience would breakout laughing.

Anna was proud of all her sons, with seven of them attending Gould's Academy and distinguishing themselves in particular ways. Jerome was known as "Jerry the Brain." After twenty years of education, he spent fifty years as a missionary and linguist in Japan and Hawaii. Jerome and Fenwicke attended college, Jerome at Bates College and Fenwicke at Colby College. Both earned A.B. Degrees and Phi Beta Kappa keys and both became Congregational ministers.

The boys were devoted to each other, and that gave them a great sense of security. The rest of the boys became farmers, one a hardware store owner, and others found their callings more suited to teaching, business, music, and oral presentations. Some excelled in sports, tennis, and football.

One year, father William purchased sheep but the winter was exceptionally harsh and the expected lambing was few. Many of the baby lambs did not survive but some that did were taken into the kitchen for warmth and feeding by the boys. The following year William purchased calves to be fed and watered by Anna and the boys. In the meantime, William went in search for employment in a lumber camp.

After ten years of struggle to meet the mortgage payments,

the farm was foreclosed on. The Holmes family of ten had to leave. In the final dealings, they came out with fifty dollars cash, with which they rented a house in the village of Lincoln. The family moved from house to house finally settling in Bethel, Maine.

But first the family experienced their first separation. The eldest boy, Walter, agreed to go to Weymouth Lumber camps to keep the books during the winter. At sixteen he was proud to be on his own and reassured his mother. William, their father, got a job with a lumber camp as chef. He had to travel to Grafton Notch, between Maine and New Hampshire. It took him two weeks to travel with a wagon and so he left his family, who would soon follow and be reunited. Anna was sad that this separation of her boys and the family as a whole had to be, but her understanding helped and it wouldn't be for long before she and the other seven boys followed to Grafton Notch, reuniting their family of nine.

Anna took her now seven boys on the train for a two-day trip to Bethel, and then there was a wagon ride with an overnight stay at an inn that provided beds but no meal. Always prepared, Anna brought food that could be prepared and enjoyed. The next morning they continued in the wagon to the Notch until they came to what appeared to be an abandoned farmhouse that was to be their home, which they would share with another family.

But at least they were near where William was cooking for the men at the lumber camp. The Holmes family set up housekeeping on one side of the house while the family of the lumber camp builder occupied the other.

Anna had two small rooms for the nine of them. The boys cut twigs from the nearby birch trees and laid them on the floor for beds. They then filled the mattresses with straw for comfort and warmth for the cold winter nights to come.

In the fall of 1893 the family moved again, to Newry Corners. There were neighbors nearby and their lives changed to picking and drying apples, enjoying a piece of rutabaga turnip once a week, and sugaring-off parties. Sugaring-off consisted of collecting a bucket of snow and ladling sap from the sugar maple trees over the top of the snow. The entire neighborhood enjoyed the fun.

In the spring the family would catch the brook trout and pick blueberries, blackberries, and raspberries for all to enjoy. In the cold winter evenings Anna would make popcorn on the stove and tell the boys stories.

In 1894 the family moved to the city of Bethel, Maine. It was one of the oldest cities in the state and a complete change from farming and lumber camps the family had experienced. They found a house on a dusty road three miles outside of town.

There were just three Protestant denomination choices of church and Anna chose the Congregationalist for her family to attend. The other two choices available were Methodist and Universalist. Each Saturday the boys were to use Anna's clothes washing tub, set it up in the kitchen, and take turns bathing.

The Eight Holmes Brothers

left to right: Luther, Charles, Ernest, Walter,
Guy, Fenwicke, Jerome, William

They each washed and ironed their own clothes so on Sunday morning they were spiffy with their hair flattened in place with sugar water. Anna, with her perfect posture, and her boys would be seen walking the three miles to the Congregationalist church in Bethel.

During the time the Holmes family lived in Lincoln, Anna and William subscribed to a Chautauqua Correspondence Course. They received a book they kept for themselves. It traveled with them through every move, while the boys had their three books. It was titled The Natural Law in the Spiritual World by Henry Drummond. The only son Anna shared the book with was William and his wife, Rose. Many years later it would be one of Ernest's favorite books.

The boys read all the books loaned to them and studied Greek and Latin, while Anna helped them with their English lessons and, particularly, mathematics. They all graduated with scores of ninety or higher.

The boys all had jobs outside of the school hours and during the summer vacations. They of course gave their earnings to Anna, who then let them keep a portion. These jobs included chores at home or in the garden or for a neighbor, cutting lawns, summer jobs in a hotel as janitors or bellboys.

Chapter Four

Fenwicke & Ernest Become Men

At his brother William's home, Ernest discovered *Emerson's Essays*. William and his wife, Rose, also had Hubbard's *Philistine* magazine available to Ernest—and anyone—to read. When Anna discovered these publications and saw Ernest creating his new understanding and philosophy for the future, she was afraid Ernest the teen (estimated to be thirteen years old) would abandon the fundamental religious beliefs he had been taught. Though Anna's beliefs were liberal to many others, she was not that open to these new ideas. She was concerned for Ernest's soul.

Anna let the incident pass and mostly forgot about it, but later in the summer when Ernest came home from the lake and brought with him a copy of the *Essays*, along with Mrs. Eddy's textbook of a new religion, Anna perked up again. But this time said she thought it was just part of his curious mind.

Ernest would read and study and practice what he believed to be a healing "formula." One of his early clients on whom he practiced treatment was his mother. For many years Anna had suffered from heart trouble. Ernest proceeded with his argument, promises in the Bible, and knowledge from other readings until he came to his understanding of the Truth. Anna subsequently lived more than forty years without experiencing any further heart problems.

In about 1910, Fenwicke, having been told by the doctor that his health problems might respond better to a warmer climate, left the Hartford Theological Society. Through the father of a student friend, he went to Ventura, California, by train for a job on a dairy. He was not happy living there and working on a dairy farm, so he moved again to live with a clergyman and his family in Pasadena in the foothills just north of Los Angeles. Fenwicke was then invited by the Superintendent of the Southern California Congregational Conference to become a home missionary in Prada, a small community near Pomona, east of Los Angeles.

Anna traveled to stay with her son in Prada and help him build a small church. During that winter he seemed to thrive. However, when summer came and the heat and unclean, smoggy air east of Los Angeles became too much, Fenwicke accepted a call from a small Congregational church in Venice, near the Pacific Ocean, where the air was fresh and clean.

The Congregational church assigned Fenwicke to be a home missionary and charged him with building a congregation. He spoke to a growing audience in a large barn-like building that had once been a bathhouse.

In 1912, twenty-five-year-old Ernest came to Venice to visit his brother and mother. He was filled with energy and had a charming personality with those sparkling, mischievous eyes. He was intelligent with an unbelievable memory, affectionate, and filled with good will for everyone.

While in Boston, Ernest had trained at the Leland Powers School of Expression as an entertainer and had traveled on the Chautauqua Circuit in New York and New England. Staying in

Ernest Holmes,
thirteen years of age

Venice, he needed a job so he put a small sign in the window of their two-bedroom, two-story home. He soon was invited to speak at a church in Pomona at the invitation from a minister friend of Fenwicke's. This experience brought him to the conclusion that this was not what he wanted to do. But Ernest stayed with Anna and Fenwicke and lived in that home for many years.

In July 1913, while Fenwicke organized his church and Ernest worked as playground director for the Grammar School, Anna assisted in the organization of the Ladies Social Circle. The group did a great amount of work locally for the needy and also raised money for Fenwicke's church.

As Ernest's ideas began to be included in Fenwicke's straight Congregationalist sermons, Anna listened and watched with wary eyes. By this time the brothers had read and studied a correspondence course by Christian D. Larsen. Larsen, a well-known author, speaker, and teacher in alignment with New Thought ideas, would one day become a part of the staff of the Institute of Religious Science and Philosophy. He was best known as the author of the *Optimist's Creed*.

The family was always close and as Ernest and Fenwicke went through their careers—creating a sanitarium in Long Beach and then selling it and buying a large home in Los Angeles, creating the *Uplift* magazine, and more family coming to California —Anna was there participating fully. It was now 1918.

After Fenwicke moved to New York, where he attracted great crowds at his lectures, he persuaded Ernest and his mother to come to New York to live and lecture with him. Anne Galer was also invited to come with them as their secretary. The pair became

Anna Holmes, seated at left, and her Red Cross Sewing Circle very well known and enjoyed crowds wherever they lectured, including Boston and Philadelphia. When the lecture season was over Fenwicke, who had fallen in love with romance novelist Katherine Eggleston, was married.

On another trip to the East Coast, Anna and Ernest invited young Reginald Armor to accompany them. They were in Lincoln, Maine, with the Holmes clan. Soon the three of them would return to Los Angeles and their large home on Third Avenue, where eleven people—friends and family—all lived. (This was in about 1919, while Reg was sixteen and still in school. When the trips included missing school, Ernest would provide a tutor.)

Anna's husband, William Nelson, however, went to Oregon, where he worked and saved money in hopes he would one day influence Anna to come to Oregon with him. That was not to be. Instead, Anna invited William Nelson to visit her and the family in Los Angeles. He did and was persuaded to stay in southern California.

The two of them remained as part of the Holmes' household on "The Hill" for the rest of their lives.

Chapter Five

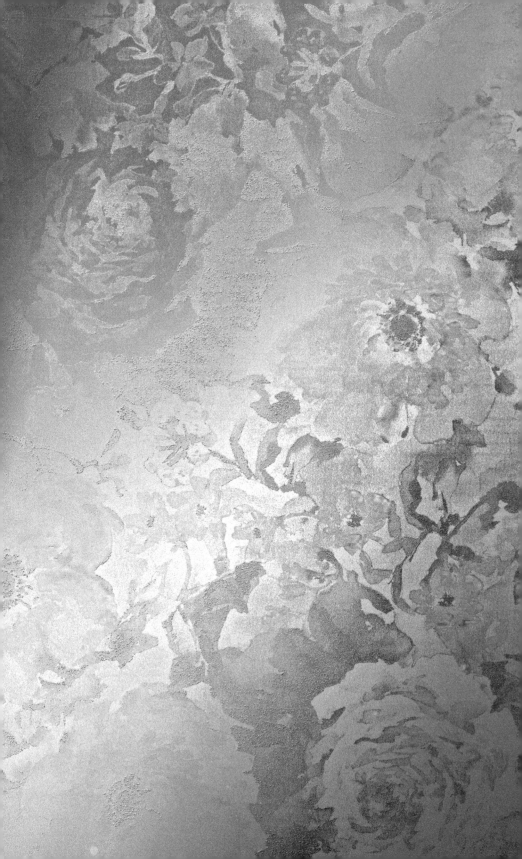

Life on The Hill

The house on "The Hill" is located in Palms, about midway between Venice Beach to the west and Los Angeles proper to the east. The property consists of three-and-a-half acres on a soft slanting hill above National Boulevard. When purchased, it had one house on the top of the hill, and Ernest's brother Guy built another next to it for his own family.

Ernest, along with his mother and father, lived in the main house, where they would live for the remainder of their lives. Years later, Guy would build another cottage down the hill a ways but still on the property for his adult son, Lawrence, and his family.

When Ernest married Hazel Foster in October 1927, she too would join the Holmes family on the "The Hill," as it came to be known. She did not like to cook nor did she pretend to enjoy housework. They hired Max to cook but he would also fill in as part-time housekeeper and sometimes chauffeur for Anna and Hazel. Ernest loved to barbecue and prepare certain dishes so he kept a watchful eye on Max.

Ernest loved working in the garden, pruning trees and bushes, and his father also participated as much as Anna and Guy would allow—and more when they weren't around. At age eighty-six, William Nelson was still hauling heavy loads in a wheel-barrow up the steep hill. But it was a bit much, and it was time for him to make his transition in the spiral of life.

It was 1933 when Ernest's father, William Nelson, and another close friend both made their transitions. A few months later Ernest was moved to write *FORE – Gleams of Eternal Life*. Anna wrote the foreword:

"Life is a school which all must attend. The same Intelligence being in each, it is the task and high privilege of the individual to so develop his God-given powers that he shall not remain in the kindergarten but may, by practical use of the lessons learned in this grade, lessons of the need of manifesting love, joy, harmony, peace, and poise, go on to each advancing grade, ever increasing in the knowledge and understanding of the One who is in all, over all, and through all, that the event called death shall be an open door to a grade beyond this plane, where he will continue to expand throughout all eternity."

— Anna Columbia Holmes

"Not long after her husband's death (roughly seven years), Grandmother Anna, then well in her eighties, sailed alone to Hawaii to spend several months in Waialua, Oahu, Territory of Hawaii, with her son Jerome..." and his family.[8] She introduced an evening ritual to her two grandsons, Jerome and Fenwicke William, and their parents of Auction Bridge, in a household that had never seen regular playing cards. They were only familiar with "Old Maid" and "Authors."

The Holmes family entertained many guests and had opportunities to meet with people of various backgrounds—scientists Albert Einstein and Dr. Robert A. Millikan of the California Institute of Technology, for example.

In 1949 Ernest and Hazel sold their home on "The Hill" to Adela Rogers St. Johns, well-known journalist and author, and a long-time and dear friend. Ernest and Hazel wanted to live closer to the Institute headquarters located at 3251 West 6th Street near Vermont Avenue. They rented a home on 6th a few blocks west of Western Avenue.

Hazel Foster Holmes, beloved
wife of Ernest

Chapter Six

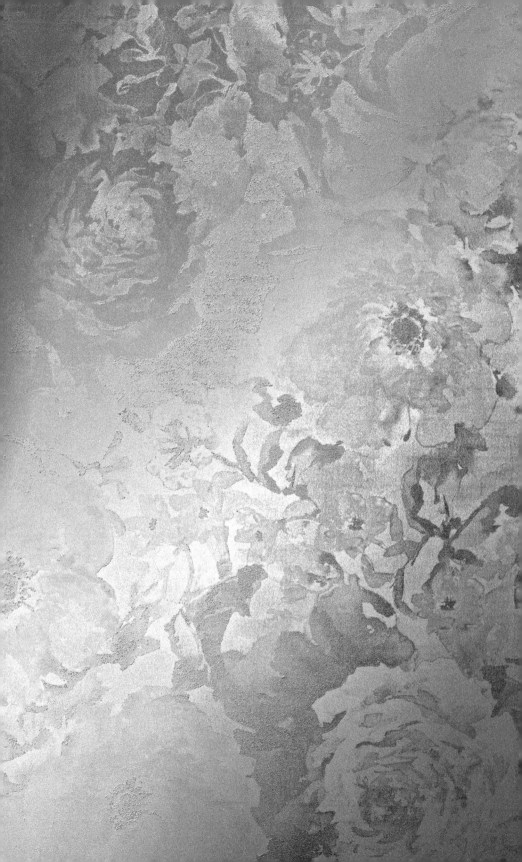

Active at the Institute

By 1921 Ernest was teaching regularly scheduled classes and lecturing in the Trinity Hotel, North Parlor, in Los Angeles. Anna and eighteen-year-old Reggie were the first practitioners. They had an office they shared, each attending to clients three alternating days a week. Reggie had only recently graduated from Venice High School, an age of "thinking he knew all the answers,"[9] and he decided after a short period of time that he was not ready and wanted to pursue other avenues of employment.

Later Ernest and Mother Anna moved the Institute office and classrooms to 2511 Wilshire Boulevard. Reggie pursued his new career, owning two confectionary stores along with his brother Edgar until the Great Depression. In 1932, Reg returned to the Institute to become a serious student and teacher along with Ernest. This relationship remained for the rest of their lives.

Anna would go to the Institute headquarters in Los Angeles with Ernest several times a week. As a practitioner, she had several clients. Over the years, Anna volunteered at the Goodwill organization and the Red Cross. She also formed the Institute Sewing Circle as a service club that gave 185,000 pieces of clothing —pre-used but now in good shape—to the poor. All through World War I and II Anna was busy knitting socks for the servicemen overseas.

Attendees of the first Practitioner's Class in 1927, Teacher Ernest Holmes, Anna C. Holmes attendee. Recorded in *The Science of Mind* textbook belonging to Isobel Ponlin.

Practitioner's Class. 1927
Teacher Ernest S. Holmes.

"Diani" Rundel

Anna C Holmes

Edith B. Macdonald.
Helen G. Lawrence.
Cora J Bamford.
Bertha S. Churchill
Vera Rosson.
Helen Van Slyke
Maud F. Huegelin
Elizabeth Cary Brubaker
Marie Frances Deal
Gertrude F. Wood
Lottie O. Park
Clara Cheshire
Gertrude M. Hallman

Isobel Ponlin — Nov Both —

W. H. Brooke

Ivy Crane Shellhamer

Mabel A. Langdon

Ida Mae Skinner,

THE SCIENCE
OF MIND

Alice R. Singleton

V. C. Winton.

O. M. Skinner

N. T. Collins

Frank Arthur Boyden

June E. Barth

Emily G. Marshall

Freda G. Smith

Anne H. Shipman

William L. Barth

Clarence Mayer

Marjorie Mayer

C. W. Mayer

A. Frances

Alberta Smith

DAILY NEWS, LOS ANGELES,

Red Cross honors elderly knitters

Los Angeles Daily News, July 16, 1942: "Industrious women over 80 who knit sweaters and socks and make other articles for the American Red Cross were complimented on their work yesterday at a tea given by the Los Angeles chapter. Mrs. C. W. Earl, 91, oldest of the guests."
(Anna Holmes, center)

For more than twenty years, from roughly 1927 to 1947, Anna, now affectionately called Mother Holmes, was the leader of the Welfare Group that met every third Thursday of the month. She would lead members in their meditation. There were many interests this group supported, one being the Children's Orthopedic Hospital.

Anna seldom missed Ernest's Tuesday Healing Meeting. She would spend many hours sitting in the library at the Institute, knitting. After some of these meetings the women would enjoy their sandwiches brought from home and lunch together in the Fiesta Room. This was in the basement and just off the parking lot in the rear of the building on 6th Street. The facility had a kitchen, providing hot coffee and a refrigerator to keep their food cool.

The Fiesta Room was the location of many parties for the Institute staff and volunteers, along with guests. During the Thanksgiving and Christmas season there would be big baskets of food to be donated, one with a turkey that would be raffled off to raise money for one of Anna's projects. On Wednesday nights, after the mid-week lecture by Ernest, Reginald Armor or one of the other ministers, the "young adults," would go to the Fiesta Room for refreshments, dancing, ping pong, and just plain fun.

In 1960, many years after her passing, Anna and her "Mother Holmes Welfare Group" were honored with a certificate of recognition for their years of service with the Los Angeles General Hospital. There was a trio of women that included Gussie Rundel, Nellie Walsh Heflin, and Anna who believed in parties for the needy. As one man was quoted as saying, "They served religion in the head and chicken and roast pork on the piano."

In the year 1945 following the end of World War II, Anna attended a very special honoring of Ernest with about six hundred people in attendance, including celebrities and notables such as Superior Judge William R. McKay and Professor Frederick P. Woeliner, the mayor of Los Angeles and the state attorney general, and Rufus von Kleinsmid, president of the University of Southern California.[10]

At age ninety-eight* Anna went to visit with another son, Jerome and his wife, now living in California, and she continued her knitting, tatting, reading, and sewing, preparing homemade gifts for Christmas. It was here that Anna made her quiet transition during the night.

After a lovely funeral service for Mother Holmes, her ashes were sent to Lincoln, Maine, and scattered over a gravesite. This site has a marker for Anna Columbia Heath Holmes next to a marker for William Nelson Holmes.[11]

* Ancestry records indicate Anna was born in 1851 rather than 1850, which would have made her ninety-eight years of age in 1949.[12]

Certificate recognizing Anna Holmes from the Los Angeles Chapter
of The American Red Cross, signed by President Harry S. Truman,
January 1946

Mother Holmes, in her nineties,
with yarn and crochet hook in hand

Epilogue

The following is taken from Anna Holmes' interview, "Zest for Living," in *Science of Mind* magazine.

"To know, and to know that you know, that God is Spirit and everywhere present, that He indwells you, in all that you really are, that when you give recognition to the God Love Incarnate, within you, It expresses Itself, thereby drawing many friends to you and causing you to feel a greater love for all those with whom you come in contact. All this is but part of the significance of Religious Science, the Science of Mind.

"When, sometimes, you feel a little weakness, a little tiredness and then give recognition from whence cometh your strength and say, 'My strength comes from the source of all strength,' and to have It respond, seems wonderful, but true.

"Then to know," she continued, "when Dear Ones leave you and go to some other place of activity, though you miss the sound of voices that you hear no more and the touch of a loving hand, you are comforted in knowing that they are very much alive and active and you say, 'God's Spirit is with them there, as it was here and will be through all Eternity.'"

Anna Columbia Holmes stayed interested in life and in sharing the Religious Science philosophy throughout her life. She wrote in her hand to Cheerio Meredith the interviewer of "Zest for Living" (August 1947, *Science of Mind* magazine) the following:

"I believe the work being done at the Institute (Institute of Religious Science, Los Angeles), by those who are keeping in mind this passage from Paul, 'Finally, Brethren, whatsoever things are true, whatsoever things are of good report, think on these things,' is of supreme importance to the world.

"The leader (Ernest Holmes) and teachers at the Institute are not only thinking on these things but are doing so with such faith and quiet enthusiasm that their import will go out into the ethers of space and join with others of the same import until the knowledge of the Lord shall cover the earth as the waters cover the sea.

"Then, indeed," she concluded, "Shall the war-drums throb no longer and the battle flags be furled in the Parliament of Man —the Federation of the World."[13]

Mother Holmes in her nineties

Footnotes

1 *Ernest Holmes: His Life and Times* by Fenwicke L. Holmes (son of Anna)

2 *Holmes' Ancestry Journal* by Fenwicke William Holmes (grandson of Anna)

3 *Ernest Holmes: His Life and Times* by Fenwicke L. Holmes

4 Ibid

5 Holmes Coat of Arms

6 *Ernest Holmes: His Life and Times* by Fenwicke L. Holmes

7 Ibid

8 *Holmes' Ancestry Journal* by Jerome Holmes

9 Taped interview with Reginald Armor, 1975

10 *Ernest Holmes: His Life and Times* by Fenwicke L. Holmes

11 *Holmes' Ancestry Journal* by Jerome Holmes

12 Ibid

13 "Zest for Living" by Cheerio Meredith, *Science of Mind* magazine, August, 1947

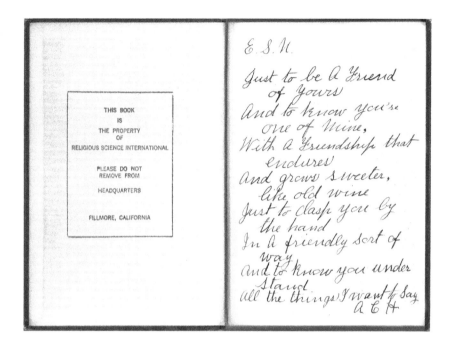

A note from Anna to Ernest written in the cover of Emmit Fox's book,
The Sermon on the Mount.

E. S. H.

Just to be a Friend of yours, And to know you're one of mine,
With a Friendship that endures, And grows sweeter, like old wine.
Just to clasp you by the hand, In a friendly sort of way,
And to know you understand, All the things I want to say.

A. C. H.

Appendix 1

Children of Anna Columbia and William Nelson Holmes

Walter Wendell Holmes, born October 22, 1876. He married Mary Lucinda Weatherbee and spent most of his life in Lincoln, Maine, where he was a shopkeeper. Walter and Mary are buried in Lincoln.

Luther Stanley Holmes, born April 21, 1878. In 1900, when the family was in Bethel, Maine, the Census of that year records that he, like his father, William Nelson, was a "hotel cook". Later he moved back to Lincoln, Maine, married Marcia Bragg Jipson and is buried in the Lincoln cemetery with his wife, who died a year earlier, and their two sons, Ellery and Rodney.

William Henry Holmes arrived on September 6, 1879. He married Rosa Martin. He was a well-traveled man, being one of the first to go to Venice, California.... In the 1930s he traveled extensively in New Zealand, coming to Maui in the Territory of

Hawaii in 1937 to be joined by his wife, Rosa, and his daughter, Anna. In Wailuku, Maui, he had a small furniture business. Later he moved back to California. He died in 1961; Rosa lived until 1972. Their youngest child, Anna Elizabeth (Holmes) Dobrick is living in Alpharetta, Georgia (2004). Her older sister Jeanette Martin (Holmes) Dickens passed away in 1989; her brother, Dennis "Bobby" Holmes, died in 1995.

Charles Holstead Holmes, born September 12, 1880. He was probably named after his great-uncle Charles Holstead Holmes, son of Samuel and Elizabeth. He married Elizabeth Kimball and moved to Massachusetts where he became a schoolteacher, dying in 1940. Their children were: Rae Verna, Bertha Northrup, and Clifton Heath. Bertha married Berle Worster. Their descendants live in Berkley, Massachusetts. Charles and Elizabeth are buried in Lincoln, Maine.

Harry Holmes was born in November 1881 and died in infancy.

Fenwicke Lindsay Holmes arrived February 6, 1883. He attended Colby College and became a prolific author, his *Law of Mind In Action* being a philosophical foundation for the metaphysical work of the Religious Science churches. He married Katherine Eggleston Junkerman, a New York author, who published a whole shelf of books about the West, in the "Zane Gray" genre, although she had hardly ever been west of the Hudson before her marriage. Her books were published under the name of Katherine Eggleston. Fenwicke died in the late 1970s.

They, too, came west to California, where they lived in Venice and Santa Monica at various times. Fenwicke traveled and lectured extensively. One of his latest books is *Ernest Holmes: His Life and Times*, which is a primary source for family lore. Not all of his assertions can be verified with genealogical accuracy, but the book is an important contribution. Fenwicke and Katherine had no children of their own but had an adopted son, Lewis Holmes.

Guy James Holmes, born May 30, 1884. He married Emma Holmes, a cousin, whose parents were Charles Robert Holmes (tenth offspring of Daniel and Charlotte [Hoyt] Holmes) and Phoebe McMonagle. Guy and Emma moved West in the general Holmes exodus from Maine and settled in Palms, California, where Guy maintained the grounds on the heavily landscaped homestead, "The Hill," where his brother Ernest also had a home. They had two children, Josephine and Lawrence.

Jerome Crane Holmes was born September 13, 1885 in Lincoln, Maine. There is some difference of opinion about this year since the records of the town clerk of Lincoln, Maine, the Archives of the State of Maine, and the book *History of Lincoln* all give the birth year of 1887. However, records of the 1900

L-R: Luther, Charles, Ernest, Walter, Guy, Fenwicke, Jerome, William

Census for Bethel, Maine, academic records from Bates College, the book *Ernest Holmes: His Life and Times*, and passport applications filled out by Jerome Crane attest to the year being 1885. Jerome married Jennie Hazel Edwards and they had two children, Jerome Knowlton and Fenwicke William.

Ernest Shurtleff Holmes, the last of the nine Holmes boys to be born, appeared on January 21, 1887. He was named after the Congregational minister in Lincoln, Maine—Ernest Shurtleff. The minister's theology was stern and rockbound stuff, which both mother Anna and father William ultimately rejected for a more liberal and forgiving theology, a pattern of belief that all of their religiously inspired sons adopted. Ernest married Hazel Gillan Foster in November 1927. They had no children. Hazel passed on May 21, 1957, and Ernest on April 7, 1960.

It was Ernest Holmes whose religious genius, organizational and oratorical gifts led to the founding, years later (1927), in California, of the Institute of Religious Science, a wide-spread community of churches and devout adherents throughout the world. Ernest's seminal book was *The Science of Mind*. His rich and inspirational life is devotedly described by his brother Fenwicke L. Holmes in his book *Ernest Holmes: His Life and Times,* which should be read by any descendant wanting a better understanding of where the Holmes family come from. (Because it is based on family lore rather than strictly conducted research, the genealogy in the book should not be taken seriously.)

Note: This information is mainly taken from the *Holmes' Ancestry Journal.*

Appendix 2

Ernest Holmes, The Mystic

Ernest, in his early years in New York, studied with Emma Curtis Hopkins. He believed that she and Meister Johannes Eckhart, the fourteenth century Dominican monk, were the greatest among all the writing mystics.

Ernest considered *The Voice Celestial* to be a treatise on mysticism. This is the way he described the experience:

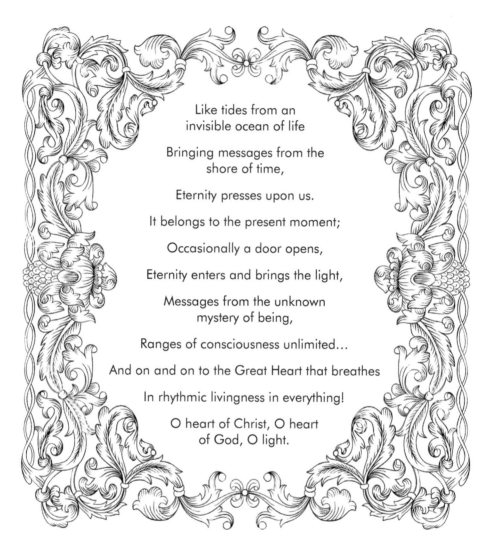

Like tides from an
invisible ocean of life

Bringing messages from the
shore of time,

Eternity presses upon us.

It belongs to the present moment;

Occasionally a door opens,

Eternity enters and brings the light,

Messages from the unknown
mystery of being,

Ranges of consciousness unlimited…

And on and on to the Great Heart that breathes

In rhythmic livingness in everything!

O heart of Christ, O heart
of God, O light.

Ernest truly believed that his life and that of every living creature was the essence of God. He discovered and lived his truth. He was often quoted as saying, "There is a Power in the Universe greater than you are, and you can use It," and, "There is one life, that life is God's Life, that Life is my life now." He lived in and as the Presence of God, a Divine Being and told us we were all in this Presence. Ernest firmly believed the Science of Mind teaching was a mystical religion.

Ernest Shurtleff Holmes was not a boy or later a man of mystery. He appeared to be quite normal with high energy, mischievous as a child, with a sparkle in his eyes that you could see was a loving spirit within him. But he was—or became—a mystic, for he had the knowledge and wisdom of truly knowing his essence as the Essence of the One of which everything is a part. He believed and accepted his Oneness with Spirit, with all of life. He could see beyond that which is seeable and hearable with our senses. He knew deep within his soul that there was only God—the living Spirit, Creator of all.

For many decades Ernest Holmes spent most of his time studying the great philosophers and subjects of art, science, religions, poetry, and everything that was of interest to him.

He wrote poetry, his ideas and thoughts about life, people, God, and their relationship to one another, and to the whole of the universe.

Ernest had an idea, and he had been writing for years, wanting to put together another great work after *The Science of Mind* (1926, edited in 1938). He had inspired ideas and writings and knew that his brother Fenwicke was an experienced author and would know how best to help bring his ideas to fruition. Together they created the epic poem, *The Voice Celestial*. Perhaps one day it will be added to the list of the greatest English literature's epic poems, alongside *The Iliad* and *The Odyssey* by Homer.

Yes, he did have a couple of back-steps, and he was aware and regretful. After his beloved wife Hazel made her transition in 1957 he greatly desired that she would come to him—communicate with him. He suffered great sorrow for the next three years, perhaps partly because he was not in her presence on that evening in May but instead at the church for a class or meeting.

For many decades Ernest had been writing about life as he saw it, his theories of involution—God—and the mystical patterns evolution—and the progress of the human and other species of life, the philosophy he had generated. Ernest worked diligently, writing his masterful poem, but he desired help in some of the basic set up and arrangement of his work, and so he went to his brother Fenwicke, then living in Oakland, California, and asked for his expertise in arranging and help completing his work. Fenwicke was also a well-known and professional author, but in some ways hung onto a few of the Congregationalist beliefs of his professional ministry. When he used words of separation, of dualism, such as sin, Ernest would remind him that he, Ernest, did not believe in sin and did not want that word in this work. In his book, *Ernest Holmes: His Life and Times*, Fenwicke Holmes brags that he snuck the word sin into *The Voice Celestial* a total of five times.

The two worked together for about two years, 1958-1959, each taking turns traveling to the other's home in northern and southern California. Finally the manuscript was finished.

THE WHITTIER EXPERIENCE

February 12, 1959

ON THIS AFTERNOON, Ernest Holmes had been invited to speak at the dedication of a church joining the New Thought organization of the Church of Religious Science in Whittier, California. As the Dean and Founder of the organization, and the philosophy of Science of Mind, Holmes was often in attendance and the main speaker at such functions. This particular day is chronicled as a special day, as all four hundred people in attendance witnessed what they believed to be and has been since called Holmes' "cosmic consciousness experience."

Ernest Holmes gave a congratulatory talk containing humor and words of encouragement and his often-repeated phrase: "There is a Power in the Universe greater than we are and we can use It; and It will multiply its effects a thousand times, in my belief, through the united consciousness of a group."

Holmes so believed in the balance of love and law and that with the teachings and living these Truth principles, God and man would unite here on Earth. As I write this account, I can feel the great building of his conviction, his voice, his being. He paraphrased from the Sermon on The Mount and stated that we, students of this philosophy, are dedicated to these truths, and he believed deeply "that everyone of us, in the secret place of the Most High, with center on his own consciousness, has the secret with the Eternal, the Everlasting, the Almighty, the Ineffable: God and I are One. And I see you doing this: And I see you uniting in one great hymn of praise, one great union of effort, one crescendo of song, and one enveloping light of consciousness."

And then there was a long pause. Holmes continued: "I see it—Oh God—the veil is thin between." Another pause, then: "We do...mingle with the hosts of heaven. I see it and I shall speak no more." *

With *The Voice Celestial* complete and having his "Whittier Experience" in February 1959, the time was nearing for Ernest to move on, and as he believed, to be with Hazel once again. The epic poem was published in 1960 and Ernest was complete April 7, 1960.

---

* The entire talk may be found in: *The Ernest Holmes Papers* as compiled by Dr. George Bendall and published by Tarcher/Penguin 2014.

Appendix 3

The Anna Holmes Fund

The United Church of Religious Science, renamed from Institute of Religious Science and later Church of Religious Science, had, as a separate and independent association, the United Clergy. Their first meeting in 1959 included Ernest Holmes and met in Santa Barbara, California, but they were to be completely independent from the corporate office. Ernest passed the following year.

During the 1980s and 1990s (the time when Dr. Marilyn Leo was active in the association) they created a special fund to help ministers in financial need, whether because of medical or family debt, or to help with travel to the annual meeting. The name of the fund was The Anna Holmes Fund.

Letters

IN KEEPING WITH THE CUSTOM of her time, Anna wrote many letters to Ernest and Hazel. Some of those letters appear here in Anna's own hand, along with a transcription. Her letters clearly demonstrate her love, her gratitude, and her understanding of her son, his wife, and their family's devotion to their work.

My dear Son,

This is your birthday. and I can hardly realize that so many years have passed since you came into manifestation on this planet: it was a wild. stormy night: toward morning as I looked on the faces of those about me I realized that they were giving up hope. and I think I never talked with God till it was then. as I thought of my little ones. I talked with Him even as we have learned since then that we could do so telling Him I could not leave these little ones alone. and He answered. also when you went out into the world while yet so young. and I saw you working so hard. when I was at your Aunt Carrie's I felt so badly. but I never told you = which perhaps I ought to have done— that you might have known that I cared = but the

BIRTHDAY NOTE TO ERNEST FROM MOTHER HOLMES —
DATE UNKNOWN

My dear Son,

This is your birthday, and I can hardly realize that so many years have passed since you came into manifestation on this planet. It was a wild, storming night. Toward morning as I looked on the faces of those about me I realized that they were giving up hope, and I think that if ever I talked with God it was then as I thought of my little ones. I talked with Him as we have learned since then that we could do so telling Him I could not leave with little ones alone. And He answered. Also when you went out into the world while yet so young and I saw you working so hard, when I was at your Aunt Carrie's, I felt so badly, but I never told you which perhaps I ought to have done—that you might have known that I cared, but the [CONTINUED] only way I seemed to know what to do was simply to tell the Father. In the years since then. I have come to believe that you was saved from the great temptations that beset those who go out into the world away from home influences - alone as it were that you had a message for the world. not only that part of the world in which you live but which reaches out - and will continue to do so beyond the boundaries of which you have never conceived. I wish you to know that my heart has always been in this work which you are doing. I am very happy in the knowledge of the good you are doing, of the help you are giving to mankind and I know more than you may realize that you talk to God. fully believing that He hears. and. that the "Inspiration of the Almighty gives you understanding" I also wish you to know how much of true happiness you have caused to come into my life and to let you know that your Father felt the same. and Guy told me when he was working on this house. that there was no other man and woman that was like you and Hazel. may you live many years. loving and being loved is my prayer for you. Mother -

only way I seemed to know what to do was simply to tell the Father. In the years since then I have come to believe that you were saved from the great temptations that had those who go out into the world away from home influences, alone as it were that you had a message for the world, not just of the world in which you live: but one which reaches out — and will continue to do so beyond the boundaries which you have never conceived. I wish you to know that my heart has always been in this work, which you are doing. I am very happy in the knowledge of the good you are doing, of the help you are giving to mankind, and I know more than you may realize that you talk to God fully believing that He heard. And "That the Inspiration of the Almighty gives you understanding" I also wish you to know how much of true happiness you have caused to come into my life and to let you know that your father felt the same. And Guy told me when he was working on this house (the Hill) that there was no other man and woman that was like you and Hazel. May you live many years caring and being loved is my prayer for you.

Mother

I hoped you will excuse any thing in this that is not worded right

(Post Script) I hoped you will excuse anything in this that is not worded right.

My dear Hazel and Ernest
another year has passed and I am
still on the pathway of life on this
planet, and at this time I wish
to thank you for the many things you
have done to make that journey
happy and most comfortable. In the
early years of this journey the road
was a bit rough and there were many
hills to climb. but you did many things
Ernest to help to level those hills. and
straighten more paths. that I was eased
of many burdens. you may have
forgotten but I have not. and
when you gave me the privilege
going with you for a time. I was
very happy. and felt like a new
person. I sometimes wonder if I
was a bit of help.. Time passed you
became successful. in your work
but you forgot neither father nor
mother. and I want you to know
that father spent the happiest years
of his life on the hill. that I know

TO HAZEL & ERNEST FROM MOTHER HOLMES
THIS IS EVIDENTLY NEAR THE END OF HER LIFE—ABOUT 1947-48.

My dear Hazel and Ernest,

Another year has passed and I am still on that pathway of life on this planet and at this time I wish to thank you for the many things you have done to make that journey happy and most comfortable. In the early years of this journey the road was a bit rough and there very many hills to climb, but you did many things Ernest to help to level those hills, and straighten those paths that I was eased of my burdens. You may have forgotten but I have not and when you gave me the privilege going with you for a time I was very happy and felt like a new person. I sometimes wonder if I was a bit of help. Time passed you became successful in your work but you forgot neither father nor mother and I want you to know that father spent the happiest years of his life on the hill. That I know [CONTINUED]

and when Hazel consented to
be a part of that life it was much
good for us; and a blessed thing
for you. I mean what word blesseth.
And one of the best for your father
and I – I have not forgotten the
care you gave to father – Hazel in his
last sickness. nor the care you have
given to me when so much sickness
I cannot help knowing it was hard
for you. had you not been the woman
you are you would have felt like
sitting down on the job. but you didn't
God. I don't know where you got your
training. but you got it. many times
I have said to myself. that I had never
seen one who would have been such
a help to Ernest – in his work he
seems to one and to others the very
foremost – he will go far and will
I believe have helped more people
to understand the meaning of
life and their relationship to life
than any one you know of

and when Hazel consented to be a part of that life

it was most good for us, and a blessed thing for you.

I mean that word blessed and one of the blessed for

your father and I. I have not forgotten the care you

gave to father Hazel in his last sickness nor the care

you have given to me thru so much sickness. I cannot

help knowing it was hard for you, had you not been

the woman you are you would have felt like sitting

down on the job, but you didn't, [thank] God. I

don't know where you got your training, but you got

it. Many times I have said to myself — that I had

never seen one who would have been such a help to

Ernest in his work, he seems at one and to others the

very foremost—he will go far and will I believe have

helped more people to understand the meaning of life

and their relationship to life than anyone you know

of [CONTINUED]

and you Hazel are a very
part of his life. step by step you
go on together in such perfect
harmony that more than one
or two of my friends and of yours
has said I like to come here. I
can feel such an atmosphere of
peace. that it helps me. Have
I written too much. I wished
you to know before I go on to
my next experience of life that
I had realized quite a good deal
of happiness in this. and you
have helped me to that realization
I think I will say good night.
and know that God bless you,
and alway will for you walk
with and talk with Him
                    mother

and you Hazel are a very part of his life. Step by step

you go on together in such perfect harmony that more

than one or two of my friends and of yours has said

I like to come here. I can feel such an atmosphere

of peace that it helps me. Have I written too much.

I wished you to know before I go on to my next

experience of life that I had realized quite a good

deal of happiness in this, and you have helped me

to that realization. I think I will say good night and

know that God blesses you and always will for you

walk with and talk with Him.

Mother

To Hazel & Ernest—
I am no writer. and
cannot express myself
as I would like too.
but I seemed to have to by
mother

Dear Hazel & Ernest—
Happy Christmas greetings.
I have no gift with
which to show my love
for you. but I give you

CHRISTMAS GREETINGS
TO HAZEL & ERNEST FROM MOTHER HOLMES
DATE UNKNOWN

To Hazel & Ernest,

*I am no writer and cannot express myself as I would
like to but I seemed to have to try.*

Mother

Dear Hazel & Ernest,

*Happy Christmas greetings. I have no gift with which
to show my love for you but I give you* [CONTINUED]

a deep and abiding
love. a wish that the
coming year may bring
to you great spiritual
and material realizations
I wish you to know
that you have made
my old age a very happy
one. I cannot express
to you how happy I
have been living

with you in a home so
harmonious. That it is
deeply felt by all. I truly
appreciate all you have done
to make my life one of
ease and enjoyment
and nothing has been
left undone to minister
to my needs in any way

a deep and abiding love, a wish that the coming year

may bring to you great spiritual and material

realizations. I wish you to know that you have made

my old age a very happy one. I cannot express to you

how happy I have been living with you in a home

so harmonious that it is deeply felt by all. I truly

appreciate all you have done to make my life one of

ease and enjoyment and nothing has been left undone

to minister to my needs in any way. [CONTINUED]

I am happy for and with
you for your success in
a work so deeply interested. a work of love and
and desire to help
others to that spiritual
realization of the true
meaning of life and their
realization of its true
meaning and I believe
you have brought comfort-
to more people than you know
I sometimes wonder where
your ideas come from.
Then I know thru medi-
tation and true commu-
ning with the source
of all Good. I believe
that Religious Science
teachings as you present it
will be known in few

I am happy for and wish you for your success in a work so deeply interested. A work of love and desire to help others to that spiritual realization of the true meaning of life and their realization of its true meaning and I believe you have brought comfort to more people than you know. I sometimes wonder where your ideas come from, what I know thru meditation and true communion with the source of all Good. I believe that Religious Science teaching as you present it will be known in far [CONTINUED]

places. and I am made.
glad in your & happy
way of presenting it.
people tell me how they
love you and I say. I
am quite fond of him
myself. I have been
made happier thru its
teachings. God bless you
He does. and always will
for you are a bringer of
good tidings of His care
and love. I am happy
that you both are so
deeply successful in
the work so dear to you.
again I say. I have no
gift but of love and
appreciation of those
so dear to me

Mother

places. And I am made glad in your happy way of presenting it. People tell me how they love you and I say I am quite fond of him myself. I have been made happier thru its teaching. God bless you. He does and always will for you are a bringer of good tiding and of His care and love. I am happy that you both are so deeply successful in the work so dear to you. Again I say, I have no gift but of love and appreciation of those so dear to me.

Mother

Dear Son.

I have no birthday day gift for you. only a great love and a deep feeling of gratitude for what you have meant to me in my life experience both spiritual and in every way that could contribute to to my comfort and happiness. When you children were young I thought that if I ever had to live to be dependent upon them it would be the hardest thing that could come to me. but you have given me such thoughtful and generous care that I have been spared that filled feeling of dependency that so many mothers have experienced but I have been made happy. and thru your generosity and thoughtfulness. and in many ways. it has made me realize more of the love bestowed upon all. from the Giver of every good that comes to Persons and while I am willing to go on to my next experience. I am very happy to be with you and with Hazel. who has added to that happiness.

Love to both of you mother

Poorly expressed but sincere.

BIRTHDAY LETTER TO ERNEST FROM MOTHER HOLMES —

DATE UNKNOWN

Dear Son,

I have no birthday gift for you, only a great love and a deep feeling of gratitude for what you have meant to one in my life experience both spiritual and in every way that could contribute to my comfort and happiness. When my children were young I thought what if I had to live to be dependent upon them, it would be the hardest thing that could come to me. But you have given me such thoughtful and generous care that I have been spared that bitter feeling of dependency that so many mothers have experienced. But I have been made happy and thru your generosity and thoughtfulness and so many ways, it has made me realize more of the love bestowed upon all from the Giver of every good that comes and while I am willing to go on to my next experience, I am very happy to be with you and with Hazel who has added to that happiness. Love to both of you.

Mother

Poorly expressed but sincere.

My dear Ernest—

I would not have you
compare the value of this little
gift with the measure of my
love for and appreciation of
the many manifestations of your
affection—not only for me but also
for the dear father who has gone on
a few days ahead, and who loved
you very dearly, and who was very
proud of you as also am I. I want
you to know that I am more

happy than perhaps you may
realize in the realization of
the good cheer you are bringing
to many people with whom
you come in contact—as well
as to—perhaps a greater number
whom you may never meet—
but who have heard you over

SENT BY ANNA TO ERNEST A FEW DAYS AFTER HIS FATHER'S PASSING, 1933

My dear Ernest,

I would not have you compare the value of this little gift with the measure of my love for and affirmation of the many manifestations of your affection—not only for me but also for the dear father who has bone on a few days ahead and who loved you very dearly and who was very proud of you as also am I. I want you to know that I am more happy than perhaps you may realize in the realization of the good cheer you are bringing to many people with whom you come in contact as well as to perhaps a greater number whom you may never meet but who have heard you over

[CONTINUED]

the radio or read some of your
books. and because of this have
come into a greater realization
of the meaning of life and their
relationship to it. at this joyous
season. as well as at all times
I give thanks that you are -
my dear son.

Mother

the radio or read some of your books and because of this have come into a greater realization of the meaning of life and their relationship to it at this joyous season as well as at all times I give thanks that you are my dear son.

Mother

About The Author

Marilyn Leo has been part of Religious Science since childhood. Her father, Reginald Armor, was very close to Ernest Holmes, beginning in the year 1915, when he was a boy of twelve, and their families remained intimate throughout Holmes' life.

Marilyn has served on many committees and served United Church (now Centers for Spiritual Living) as director of the World Ministry of Prayer, Ecclesiastical Officer/Vice President, Organizational Renewal Project, chair of what is now the Global Ministries, as well as president, secretary, and treasurer (at different times) for the Wisdom Council (retired ministers' association). She has received several special recognitions, including the "Living Treasure Award" given by her ministerial colleagues. In 2009, Marilyn received the "Golden Heart Award," also given by the United Clergy of Religious Science. United Church has honored her with honorary Doctor of Divinity and Doctor of Religious Science recognitions.

Though retired from the usual ministerial duties, she founded the Science of Mind Archives and Library Foundation, and presently serves on the Board of Trustees for The Hefferlin Foundation, an independent nonprofit foundation supporting the teaching of Science of Mind. In that capacity she is secretary of the board and co-chair of the Education/Scholarship Committee.

Marilyn is the author of *Chronicles of Religious Science, Volumes I and II.* Besides her book *In His Company: Ernest Holmes Remembered,* she has written articles for *Science of Mind* and *Creative Thought* magazine, contributed the manuscript for *That Was Ernest* written by her father, Dr. Reginald Armor, and published by DeVorss & Company. She compiled and edited *Love and Law* published by J. Tarcher/Putnam/Penguin, and she wrote the foreword for John Waterhouse's book *Five Steps to Freedom,* which, incidentally, has been translated to Spanish and Russian and has become required reading for some Science of Mind classes. It is also being created as an audiobook.

Marilyn has been working in the Religious Science Archives for twenty years and created the Archives and Library Foundation, a non-profit organization that houses all archival information for Centers for Spiritual Living. It is a "living archives" in that there are constantly additions being made. Visit the website:

www.ScienceofMindArchives.com

SCIENCE OF MIND®

ARCHIVES & LIBRARY FOUNDATION

Where the Past Illuminates the Future

CPSIA information can be obtained
at www.ICGtesting.com
Printed in the USA
LVHW070239220221
679524LV00006B/698